M000306356

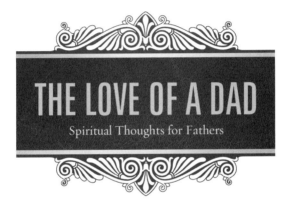

THE LOVE OF A DAD

Spiritual Thoughts for Fathers

JAMES W. MOORE

Abingdon Press

NASHVILLE

THE LOVE OF A DAD
SPIRITUAL THOUGHTS FOR FATHERS

Copyright © 2013 by Abingdon Press
All rights reserved.

Library of Congress Cataloging-in-Publication Data has been requested.

ISBN 978-1-4267-6745-6

Scriptures quotations marked (NRSV) are taken from the New Revised Standard Version of the Bible, copyright 1989, Division of Christian Education of the National Council of the Churches of Christ in the United States of America. Used by permission. All rights reserved.

13 14 15 16 17 18 19 20 21 22—10 9 8 7 6 5 4 3 2 1

MANUFACTURED IN THE UNITED STATES OF AMERICA

CONTENTS

HE CALLED GOD "FATHER"

When we really stop to think about it, it's amazing, inspirational, and challenging. I am talking about the fact that when Jesus grew up and got ready to say the very best thing he could think of to say about God, he said God is like a loving, gracious, compassionate, understanding, supportive father. He called God "Father"!

What a compliment this is to Joseph! I think it is safe to say that much of what Jesus learned as a child and as a young person, he learned from Joseph. Joseph must have been a good father because Jesus called God "Father" and that was obviously a good image in his mind.

Jesus felt Joseph's love; he saw his grace and compassion, his mercy and kindness; he experienced his strong support and parental care, and then Jesus said: "God is like that! God is like a loving parent! God cares for his children the way Father Joseph cares for Me!"

In thinking of this as I write this book, I realized something very significant: specifically, that the good news of our Christian faith is that God claims all of us as children! That's what Jesus taught us, perhaps in large part because he must have had a very special relationship with his father, Joseph.

Tragically, some children today do not have a good relationship with their fathers, and consequently, the "father image" is not a good one for them. They literally cringe at the word *father*, because it brings to their minds destructive, dysfunctional, even painful memories, and that is so sad. Well, all we can say about that is shame on those fathers for messing up on one of the most important jobs God has given us in this world: the awesome job of being a dad to our children.

When that father-child relationship is right, it is so beautiful, so precious, and so inspiring, and that, evidently, is the kind of relationship Jesus experienced with his earthly dad, Joseph, because Jesus paid Joseph the highest possible tribute. He reflected on Joseph's love, support, and gracious generosity, and he said, "God is like that! God is like a loving father!"

What an inspiration that is to us who are dads today—and what a challenge! Have your children ever looked at you—the way you act, the way you care, the way you understand, the way you listen, the way you help, the way you love—then said to themselves: "That's what God is like!" That's what Jesus did with regard to his earthly dad, Joseph, and that's one big reason Jesus called God "Father."

It is my hope and prayer that as we who are dads today experience this book together, we will be stirred, challenged, and inspired by the presence and power of the Holy Spirit to be better Christians, better disciples, and better dads!

ONE

A FATHER'S GREAT FAITH

Luke 8:49-56

It all started on a Sunday afternoon in the month of May. My father quite suddenly became terribly ill with a ruptured appendix. I was twelve years old at the time. He had always been hale and hearty and healthy, the strength of the family. He was rushed to the hospital. My brother (age fourteen), my sister (age six), and I stayed home with our grandmother and waited anxiously for some word. About an hour or so later, the chaplain from Methodist Hospital (who had formerly been our pastor) knocked on our front door and told us that there had been an accident, a car wreck, that both of our parents were injured and had been admitted to the hospital, and that we should come with him.

We went to the hospital, but we couldn't find out much, just that our mother was being cared for in the emergency room and that our father was in surgery. We walked the floor at the hospital and prayed in the chapel for several hours before we were sent home for the night.

Shortly after my brother, my sister, and I had fallen asleep, the call came from the hospital that our father had died. Even though I was only twelve,

I have several very vivid images of that tragic event in our lives. First, when the call came, the relatives who had gathered decided to let the children sleep. They felt it would be best to let us get a good night's rest and then tell us the bad news in the morning. But what they didn't count on was that I got up early and went out to get the morning paper. When I opened it up, there on the front page was the picture of our smashed-up car and the caption beneath announcing that my dad had died in the car wreck.

Before anyone could tell me, I had read it in the newspaper. I remember as if it were yesterday—sitting in the living room of our home early that Monday morning with the newspaper spread across my lap and the relatives coming in and seeing me and not knowing what to say. And I remember even in my shock and grief feeling sorry for them.

Another vivid image that would change my life forever came that night at the funeral home. As we stood there by my dad's casket, hundreds of people came by. Some were rich, some were poor, some were young, and some were old. Some were African Americans, some were Anglo Americans, some were Asian Americans, some were Mexican Americans, some were professional people, some were uneducated laborers, some were unemployed, some I knew quite well, and some I had never seen before. But they all came. They came over and spoke to us and expressed their sympathy, and every one of them said the same thing to me: "Jim, your dad was kind to me."

Now, they didn't all use those exact words, but each one in his or her own way said the same thing: "Jim, your dad was kind to me." Even though I was just twelve years old at the time, I made up my mind then and there that the best tribute I could pay to my dad was to take up his torch of kindness, to somehow with the help of God let his kindness live on in me, to keep his special brand of kindness alive and well in the world through me, to pass his kindness on to everybody I met. And from that moment I have tried my best to be a kind person. There are a lot of things I'm not, but since that day I have tried, as a tribute to my earthly father and my heavenly Father, to be a kind person. I haven't always succeeded, but I have tried and I am still trying to let my father's kindness live on in me. You see, I know what kindness is because Wendell Moore was my father! And I have learned even more what kindness is because Jesus Christ is my Savior. The best tribute I can pay my dad and the best tribute I can pay my Christ is to keep their spirit of kindness alive and well in this world.

In similar fashion, the daughter of Jairus was able to say later in her life, "I know what great faith is because Jairus was my father." In the gospel of Luke, chapter 8, we find the story. Jairus was the ruler of the synagogue. He was a man of substance—rich, powerful, and religiously prominent. In the synagogue, he called the shots. He represented the elite of society, especially in the religious world, and given his position, he probably would not normally have given much time or thought to this traveling teacher from Nazareth called Jesus.

But crisis came. The angel of death hovered over Jairus's house. Jairus's twelve-year-old daughter became critically ill. It looked hopeless. She was dying. As Jairus stared the potential death of his daughter in the eye, he became a different man. He became a desperate man. He swallowed his pride. He pushed the rules aside, and he ran to Jesus for help!

Let me put a footnote here. By this time, many of the synagogues were closed to Jesus. Many of the religious leaders were suspicious of Jesus. They didn't want to be associated with him because so many of them saw him as an untrained troublemaker who was upsetting the people.

Jairus may well have been one of those "doubting detractors," but then his daughter got sick, she was dying, and Jairus (loving father that he was) threw caution to the wind and ran to Jesus for help! He fell down at the feet of Jesus and pleaded with the Master to come to his house, because his only daughter was gravely ill and dying. Jesus went with him. He healed a sick woman along the way. And then messengers came from Jairus's house telling him that his daughter had died. "It's too late. She's gone. No need to trouble the Master anymore." But Jesus said to him, "Don't be afraid. Just believe and she will be made well."

They go on to the house. The people are weeping and mourning. They scoff at Jesus for even thinking he can do anything about this. But Jesus goes in to that little girl, and he resurrects her. He loves her back to life, and then (I love this) he tells them to give her something to eat.

Now there are many beautiful lessons in this story in Luke 8, but I want to look closely with you at the faith of this father. Three things stand out.

HIS FAITH WAS ACTIVE

There is a fascinating story about a naive villager who was born and reared in a remote community. One day he traveled to the big village for the first time. He obtained lodging at an inn and during the night was awakened by the loud beating of drums. He asked what all the drum beating was about. He was told that it meant a fire had broken out in the village, and the beating of the drums was the city's fire alarm.

When he got back home, he quickly told the village

leaders about what he had learned in the big village. "They have a wonderful and effective system in the big city. When a fire breaks out, the people beat their drums and before long the fire goes out."

Well, as you can imagine, this excited the village authorities greatly. So they ordered a large supply of drums and distributed them to the people. When a fire broke out, there was a deafening sound of drums beating everywhere. The villagers anxiously beat their drums and waited for the flames to die down and go out, but to their surprise and dismay, the fire did not go out and there was much destruction. About that time a sophisticated traveler from the big village was passing through. "What's going on?" he asked. When he was told how they had beat their drums and beat their drums and still the fire had not gone out, he said, "Oh, no! You misunderstood. Do you really think a fire could be put out by beating drums? The drums don't put out the fire. They only sound the alarm for the people to wake up and to take action to extinguish the flames."

This is a valuable parable for the church. It shows that the beating of the religious drums of ritual and rhetoric will not solve our social ills or bring healing to our troubled world. It's not enough to just beat the drums; we have to actively do something. The weepers and wailers had come to Jairus's house to mourn the death of his daughter. This was a part of their culture. Professional weepers came to cry loudly, to play mournful-sounding flutes, and to tear their garments as signs of respect for the one who was dead or dying. But Jairus could not content himself with that. He sprang into action. He ran to get help. He ran to bring the Great Physician there to heal his daughter.

The point is clear. The Christian faith is not just a creed we profess; it is a lifestyle we actively practice. It's not enough to beat the drums or talk a good game.

We have to walk the walk and actively live the faith. Jairus's faith was strong that day because it was active.

HIS FAITH WAS HOPEFUL

Everybody else had caved in and given up, but Jairus would not quit. He kept on hoping, and he placed his hope in the right one.

Some years ago, during the Great Depression in our country, a group of leaders gathered in Chicago to address the burdensome problems facing the people of our nation. These leaders went to an African American church on the south side of Chicago. People from the neighborhood came in to discuss their woes and problems as they tried to survive the Great Depression—no jobs, little money, big bills, sagging morale.

Among the leaders who went to see how they might help these people were Charles Gilkey of the

University of Chicago and Clarence Darrow, the famous agnostic attorney. Clarence Darrow decided to take advantage of the situation to dramatically underscore the plight of black Americans. He said to them, "You have no jobs; you have no money; you have no power; you have no opportunity." He then ended by saying, "And yet you sing. No one can sing like you do! There's something I don't understand, and I want to ask you about it. What in the world do you have to sing about?"

There was silence in the room, and then the voice of an elderly African American woman came from somewhere in the back of the hall: "We've got Jesus to sing about!" Oh yes, we have lots of problems, but we also have Jesus, and he is what we sing about. For once in his life, Clarence Darrow was stopped dead in his tracks. He was face-to-face with people who had faith and hope in Jesus.

If you and I could somehow get into a time machine and go back to that scene in Jairus's house in the first century, we would probably hear the people saying to Jairus something like this: "It's hopeless, Jairus. We've done all we can. It's no use. We're so sorry, but all hope is gone." I can just hear Jairus answering, "No! Jesus is near. He can help. He can bring healing. He is our hope."

That's the good news of our faith, isn't it? We can always be people of hope because Jesus is near. We've got Jesus to sing about.

Jairus expressed a great faith that day because he refused to quit, he refused to give up. First, his faith was active, and second, his faith was hopeful.

HIS FAITH WAS TRUSTING

Even after word came to Jairus that his daughter had died, he kept on trusting Jesus.

One of the warmest memories of my childhood was something that happened to me when I was five years old. I had spent the day with my grandmother. Toward evening, a fierce storm hit. "Oh, Jim," my grandmother said, "How in the world are we going to get you home in this weather?" The answer came moments later as my dad walked in the front door. He had come to get me.

The storm showed no signs of letting up. The wind was blowing hard, rain was pelting down, lightning was flashing in the sky, thunder was rumbling behind the clouds. It was a dark and scary night. We didn't have far to go to get to our house, but the storm was nasty and getting worse. My dad had on a big navy blue all-weather coat, and as we got ready to leave my grandmother's home, he said, "Jim, come under here." He covered me with his coat, he picked me up, and out into the storm we went.

Even though it was raining hard and the wind was howling and I couldn't see a thing under that coat, I was not afraid at all. Why? Because I knew my father could see where we were going. So I just held on tightly and trusted him. Soon the coat opened, and we were safely home.

Death is like that for the Christian. Grief is like that. The problems and challenges of life are like that, too, for the Christian. God covers us with protective love. God holds us up and guides us through the storm. Sometimes in this life there is no way around it. We have to walk through the pain, the storms, the heartache. But the good news of the Christian's faith is this: we never walk alone. God is with us and will see us through.

Jairus knew that, and that's why he had a great faith, a faith that was active, a faith that was hopeful, and a faith that trusted Christ. That's the kind of faith we all need, isn't it?

TWO

TEACHING OUR CHILDREN TO LOVE

Matthew 19:14

Some years ago, I asked some young children in Sunday school what Father's Day meant to them. One little boy answered: "It's just like Mother's Day, except you don't spend as much money for the present." Someone once defined a father by saying: "He's a man who has replaced the cash in his wallet with snapshots."

Recently, I ran across a beautiful prayer about dads. Let me share it with you:

Menders of toys,

Leaders of boys,

Changers of fuses,

Kissers of bruises.

Bless Them, O Lord, Bless Them.

Movers of couches,

Soothers of ouches,

Pounders of nails,

Tellers of tales.

Bless Them, O Lord, Bless Them.

Hangers of screens,

Counselors of teens,

Fixers of bikes,

Friends of tykes.

Bless Them, O Lord, Bless Them.

Rakers of leaves,

Cleaners of eaves,

Dryer of tears,

Comforters of fears.

Bless Our Fathers, O Lord, Bless Them.

[attributed to Jo Ann Heidbreder]

Now, let me raise a dramatically important question in this chapter that we who are dads ought to think long and hard about, namely, this: how do we teach our children to be loving people? Let me prime the pump of our thinking with this illustration. Our granddaughter, Sarah, is a delightful personality who is never at a loss for words. When she was five years old, her mother took her to a public playground. Sarah immediately began to play with two other little girls on the playground equipment. The two other girls were three or four years older than Sarah, and they were sisters.

As they were playing, the older sister got upset with her younger sister and she said to her with anger, "You are stupid and ugly."

When Sarah heard that, she said: "Word Police! Word Police!"

The older girl turned to Sarah and said, "What did you say?"

Sarah said, "Word Police."

The older girl retorted, "Why did you say that?"

Sarah answered, "I said 'Word Police' because you said two bad words."

"What bad words did I say?" the older girl asked her.

Sarah responded, "You said *stupid* and *ugly,* and

those are bad words, and when you say bad words, the 'word police' come out!"

"Oh yeah?" said the older girl. "Well, how about @#$%?" and she blurted out a four-letter word that I would not say anywhere.

And Sarah said, "Yep! I think that would be one too!"

Now, what is interesting about that true-life experience at that public playground is this: we see that one child was being taught daily how to be loving, gracious, and respectful toward others and also how to stand tall for what is right and good. She had learned at home and at church that it is not nice to call someone "stupid" or "ugly." On the other hand, the other child's parents were sitting right there on a park bench within easy earshot of that colorful conversation. They were reading magazines. They never looked up. They never said a word. They never corrected their daughter.

In recent years, psychologists have emphasized strongly how tremendously important those early years are. Our personalities, our attitudes, our values, our habits, our principles, our self-esteem, even our IQs are shaped so powerfully by what happens to us in those first few years of early childhood.

Some years ago at the end of vacation Bible school in our church, the quote of the week came from one of our four-year-olds, who said: "I like Bible school at St. Luke's better than Thanksgiving, Valentines, and Chucky Cheese Pizza!" Now, that's saying something. In one Bible school paper, there was an article that touched my heart. It was called "A Child's Appeal," by Ezekiel Moiben, and it had these poignant words:

I am a child. All the world awaits my coming.

All the earth watches with interest to see what I shall become. . . .

You hold my destiny in your hands.

You determine largely whether I shall succeed or fail.

Give me, I pray, these things that make for happiness.

Train me, I beg you, that I may be a blessing to the world.

Well, how do we do that? How do we train our children that they may be a blessing to the world? How do we crown their heads with wisdom and fill their hearts with love, and set them on the right paths? What are the best things we can do for and give to our children?

Not long ago, a fourteen-year-old girl was suspended from school for cheating. When her mother tried to talk to her about it, the girl screamed, "So what? Life's different now. You're so old-fashioned. We don't go by your rules anymore."

"I guess that's true," the shaken mother said to me later. "And I don't know how to cope with it."

Well, is that true? Can it be in this troubled, stressful, hectic, fast-changing, pressure-packed world in which we live that the rules have changed? Have the values changed so that we don't know what to teach our children anymore? Do we just improvise as we go along? Of course not! No matter how fast times may change, no matter how much customs may change, certain qualities always abide, certain values always endure, certain truths are always relevant, certain attitudes are always appropriate, certain actions are always right.

What are these enduring values? I have thought about this a long time, and I couldn't begin to list them all, but here are a few to try on for size. I'm sure you will think of others.

THERE IS HONESTY

The apostle Paul put it like this: "Love does not rejoice in what is wrong; it rejoices in what is right."

We need to teach our children that integrity matters, that honesty is so important! Nothing will ever change the need for honesty. In fact, it is impossible to imagine any livable society without it. Integrity is the quality of being able to be trusted. It means that we don't lie to each other, that we will do what we say we will do, that the affection we profess is genuine and the praise we give is honest.

To teach children to grow up to be like that is sometimes difficult because honesty and integrity seem sometimes to be in short supply. "I'm so ashamed," the man said. "My teenage son has been helping a friend fix up a secondhand car, and the other day he told us how he had helped sell it too. Know what he said? He said, 'Hey Dad, I showed Brian that neat trick with the mileage you used when you got rid of the old Chevy.' " You see, we teach our children honesty (or dishonesty) by the way we ourselves live.

A little six-year-old boy was in the drugstore. He saw a comic book that he really wanted, but he only had a nickel. So when the storekeeper was not looking, he took the book. His parents found out and discussed what to do. Of course, they agreed, it had to be paid for, but could they just take the money to the store and explain? After all, he's just a very little boy, and if they talked to him about it, they were certain he would never do it again. But no, they couldn't settle for that. They couldn't treat it that lightly, and finally, a little six-year-old boy, accompanied by his parents, went back to the store and told the owner what he had done, paid for the book, and asked for forgiveness. Those parents were right!

Honesty and integrity do not come without a price, and that lesson is best taught when children are young. First of all, there is honesty.

THERE IS LOVE

Remember what the apostle Paul said about love. He called it the greatest of all, the best way of all. We need to give our children love, and lots of it. And we need to show them how to be loving persons, how to make love the theme of their lives and their stance toward the world.

In his book *The Miracle of Love*, Dr. Charles Allen tells about a man who consulted a noted psychiatrist about the best things he could do for his children. He made a list: give them the best material things, the best education, good religious training, travel, culture, and social etiquette.

The psychiatrist said: "All these are extremely important, but you have left out the most important thing you can do for your children." The man wondered aloud what he had not named. The psychiatrist replied: "The best thing you can do for your children is to love their mother!"

The best way to teach children how to be loving persons is to model love, to exemplify love, to live love in front of them, to teach love not only in words but in our own actions. Honesty and love—what wonderful gifts to give our children—but there is one other to be added, the one that holds them all together and makes honesty and love possible.

THERE IS FAITH

Faith is not a small room stuck on the back of the house that we visit every now and then. It is the

LIGHT in all the rooms. Faith enables us to be honest and loving. It's the golden thread that ties it all together. It is the cement that gives strength and endurance against the storms of life. It's the solid foundation, the undergirding, the strong rock.

Dads, tune in closely now (granddads too): if you want to teach your children faith, the best way to do that is to let them see and experience your faith. Of course, teach them memorized prayers, but remember it's more important for them to see you pray and to hear you pray. Of course, encourage them to attend church and Sunday school, but remember it's even more important for them to see you excited to be there.

Dr. Dick Murray was one of the leading Christian educators in America. He taught at Perkins School of Theology at Southern Methodist University. He once came to our church to speak to our teachers, and I will never forget something he said that night. He told about teaching his four-year-old grandson Martin the Gloria Patri. He said he had taught Martin "Old Mac-Donald" and "Row, Row, Row Your Boat," and decided that he needed to teach little Martin the Gloria Patri. So they got in the car, buckled up, and rode through the streets of Dallas singing:

> Glory be to the Father and to the Son and to the Holy Ghost;
> as it was in the beginning, is now, and ever shall be,
> world without end. Amen. Amen.

At the top of their lungs, granddaddy, Dick Murray, and grandson, Martin, sang the Gloria Patri over and over and over, and they had a marvelous time. A short time later, they took Martin to "big church" for the first time, and when they got to that place in the service where the congregation stood together and began to sing boldly the Gloria Patri, Dick Murray said he felt a tug on his coat. Martin was doing the tugging and motioning for his granddad to bend down so he could tell him something. Dick Murray bent down and four-year-old Martin said excitedly in his ear: "Poppa! Poppa! They are singing our song. They are singing our song."

What are the best things we can give our children? I'm sure there are many good answers to that question. But high on every list should be honesty, love, and faith. Jesus said, "Let the little children come to me, and do not stop them; for it is to such as these that the kingdom of heaven belongs" (Matthew 19:14).

THREE

THE GREATEST OF THESE

1 Corinthians 13:13

Not long ago, some friends gave me a copy of a wonderful magazine article entitled "The World According to Student Bloopers," written by Richard Lederer of St. Paul's School. It's a humorous list of student bloopers collected by teachers of children and youth from all across the United States. Listen now to actual quotes from essays and tests.

"Jacob was a man in the Bible who stole his brother's birth mark."

"Socrates was a famous Greek teacher who went around giving people advice. They poisoned him, but actually Socrates died from an overdose of wedlock."

"Gravity was invented by Isaac Walton. It is chiefly noticeable in the Autumn when the apples are falling off the trees."

"Benjamin Franklin went to Boston carrying all his clothes in his pocket and a loaf of bread under each arm. He invented electricity by rubbing cats backwards and declared, 'A horse divided against itself cannot stand.' Franklin expired in 1790 and later died for this."

Now, it is obvious from these classic student bloopers

that sometimes we miss the message. Sometimes we stop short of the full truth and consequently end up with distorted or strange answers. Sometimes we "sort of" learn something but don't quite get it right. If we are not careful, we can just play around the edges of truth and somehow miss the main point. This is precisely what 1 Corinthians is all about. Here, Paul is underscoring the crucial truth, the main point.

The apostle Paul had founded the church there in Corinth in about AD 50, and he had stayed with them for about eighteen months. But then, when he moved on to work in Ephesus, he kept getting these disquieting reports of trouble in the Corinthian church. As long as he had been there with them, everything went nicely, but when he left, all kinds of problems broke out. Conflicts and cliques, divisions and dissensions, party strife and power struggles were tearing the church apart. Jealousy, self-righteousness, greed, hostility, and arrogance were running rampant—all in the name of religion!

How could this happen? Well, the Corinthians had gotten a taste of religion, but they had missed the main point! So, like a father teaching his children, the apostle Paul dealt with the Corinthians. First, he examined their problems (for twelve chapters he dissects their mistakes and misunderstandings), and then he shows them a better way!

"Now, look! Here it is!" he says to them. "This is what it's all about! Here is the secret! You want the key to life? Well, here it is for you!" And he launches into 1 Corinthians 13, the love chapter.

If I speak in the tongues of mortals and of angels, but do not have love, I am a noisy gong or a clanging cymbal. And if I have prophetic powers, and understand all mysteries and all knowledge, and if I have all faith, so as to remove mountains, but do not have love, I am nothing. . . .

Love is patient; love is kind; love is not envious or boastful or arrogant or rude. It does not insist on its own way; it is not irritable or resentful; it does not rejoice in wrongdoing, but rejoices in the truth. It bears all things, believes all things, hopes all things, endures all things. . . .

And now faith, hope, and love abide, these three; but the greatest of these is love. (vv. 1-2, 4-7, 13)

Powerful, moving, majestic words, but what is Paul communicating here really? He is saying the same thing Jesus said again and again: love is the key. Love is the one thing that is always right. Love is the major ingredient in a happy family. Love is the most authentic sign of discipleship and spiritual maturity.

Love is the single most powerful thing in all the world. Love is the most dramatic evidence of God's powerful presence in our lives. If we miss love, we miss the main point—and we miss God!

So what better thing could we do than think together about this question: how do we teach our children to be loving persons? You'll recall that we began that conversation in the last chapter. Recently, I asked a number of people that question, and interestingly, they all gave the same answer. They all said: "By example!" That's a good answer. Let's break it down a bit and see if we can find ourselves or our children somewhere between the lines.

WE CAN TEACH OUR CHILDREN TO BE LOVING BY THE EXAMPLE OF RESPECT

Recently, I was standing in line in a supermarket. There was a family in front of me who got into a rather heated argument. I never cease to be amazed at how some people talk to their children. As I overheard these parents unload this vicious verbal attack on their child, I thought to myself that they wouldn't talk to a roach like that with those ugly words and in that hostile, venomous tone of voice.

Horrible expletives, dirty names, profane accusations, nasty insinuations, and angry put-downs were all aimed directly at a tired little boy who just wanted a piece of bubble gum. Maybe he didn't need the bubble gum, but even when we say no, we can say it with respect, can't we? We need to always remember that every child is a child of God, a human being, a person of integrity and worth, a person for whom Christ came and died. One of the ways we teach our children to be loving persons is by being patient with them, understanding of them, and respectful toward them in every stage of their lives.

I once ran across an article that had appeared originally in a Dutch magazine. It's called "How Fathers Mature," but it's really about the many different transitions children go through over the years as they assess their fathers.

I'm 4 years old and my Daddy can do anything.

I'm 7 years old and my Dad knows a whole lot.

I'm 9 years old and Dad doesn't know quite everything.

I'm 12 years old and Dad just doesn't understand.

I'm 14 years old and Dad is so old-fashioned.

I'm 17 years old and the man is out of touch and out to lunch.

I'm 25 years old and Dad's okay.

I'm 30 years old: I wonder what Dad would think about this.

I'm 35 years old: I must get Dad's input first.

I'm 50 years old and wonder what would Dad have thought about that.

I'm 60 years old and I sure wish I could talk it over with Dad once more.

They will go through stages and they may go off on tangents, but if we respect our children and if they see us treating every person we meet with dignity and respect, with kindness and courtesy, they will learn to love, and most often, they will work through the stages, the fads, the peer pressures, the transitions and eventually they will come back to the values of their parents, to the principles and the standards of their home, and to the art of love.

We can teach our children to love by the example of respect.

WE CAN TEACH OUR CHILDREN TO BE LOVING PERSONS BY THE EXAMPLE OF SACRIFICE

People who have been forced by circumstances to sacrifice for each other have a special tenderness toward each other. Two army buddies who have been forced to share their rations or their canteen of water in a difficult time never forget each other. There is something about sacrificing together that creates love.

A few years ago, I spoke at a college graduation exercise. Something happened that day I will never forget: one young woman, when she received her diploma, broke out of line and walked about halfway into the audience and handed the diploma to her parents. Then she hugged them both tightly, and they all cried together tears of joy. Her parents looked a little tired. Their clothes were not the latest style. I never knew for sure why that young graduate did that, but I suspect that through that act she was saying, "We did it together. You deserve this too. I have come to this place because of you. I know how you've sacrificed for me." It was a powerful demonstration of love. Sacrifice creates Love!

First, there is respect. Second, there is sacrifice.

WE CAN TEACH OUR CHILDREN TO BE LOVING PERSONS BY THE EXAMPLE OF CHRIST

The best thing we can do for our children is to introduce them to Jesus Christ. If we help them accept Christ into their lives as a powerful presence if they catch his spirit from us, that more than anything else will make them genuine, loving persons. But it has to be more than a vague nod in his direction. It has to be a personal relationship, a constant and ongoing closeness, a warm and lively friendship, a deep and unshakable commitment.

During World War II, a young man went overseas. A few days after he left, his wife gave birth to a baby boy. For three years, that young soldier served in the South Pacific, and he never saw his son until the war was over. The wife tried to bridge the problem of separation by practicing a little ritual each night as she put the child to bed. Each evening they would put on his pajamas, kneel beside the bed to say their prayers, and then the little boy would run over to a framed picture of his father on the bed table, kiss the picture of his dad, and then run back and tumble into bed. This nightly ritual went on for three years.

Then the day came—the father returned from the war. That night, for the first time, Dad got to participate in the bedtime ritual. He helped his son put on his pajamas. Then mother, father, and son knelt together beside the bed for prayer, and when the prayers were completed, his mother said, "Now you can kiss your father goodnight." Can you imagine what happened? That's right. The little boy ran over to the nightstand, kissed his father's picture, ran back, and tumbled into bed, leaving his dad standing there with open, empty arms!

Now, of course, over time the little boy understood. He came to know his dad as a person, as a living presence and not just a picture. But that's a parable for us, isn't it? Many people today in their religious experience are still merely kissing the picture. They haven't really accepted the living Christ into their lives. They don't really know him personally yet. They just kiss the picture.

The point is clear: if we want our children to be loving persons, we can teach them how to love by showing them respect and sacrifice and by introducing them to Christ. He will not only teach them to love, he will love them and he will love through them!

FOUR

THE MANY FACES OF LOVE

1 Corinthians 13:1-13

I heard Bill Cosby say once that he was twenty years old before he realized that over the years when his father said things like "stand up straight, tie your shoes, clean up your room, eat your vegetables," what he really meant was "I love you."

With that in mind, let me share with you an article attributed to Erma Bombeck titled "The Trouble with Father." In it she talks about how her mother was always there for her, but her father had a problem with showing love. For instance, he made her return a stolen candy bar and 'fess up to what she'd done. But her mother understood that she was "just a kid." He would run errands at her birthday parties, but it was her mom who entered with the beautiful cake. When she broke her leg, her mother held her all the way to the hospital and carried her in while her father dropped them off at the door and then went to park the car. She goes on:

> When I got married, it was Mom who got all choked up and cried. He just blew his nose loudly and left the room.

All my life he said, "Where are you going? What time are you coming home? Do you have gas in the car? Who's going to be there? No, you cannot go." Not Mom. She just loved me, but Daddy, he just didn't know how to show love unless . . . Oh, my goodness, is it possible? Is it possible he showed it all along and I didn't recognize it?

Well, the point of that poignant and beautiful story is clear. There are many faces of love. There are many different ways to express love and show love.

This is what the apostle Paul is underscoring in 1 Corinthians 13. Here in the love chapter he reveals in a powerful way that love is, indeed, a many-splendored thing. Love has many sides and many faces.

Paul begins this chapter by demonstrating the importance of love in a striking way. In effect, he says:

"No matter what you say or do, if it's not purified by love, it's not worth anything!"

Then in the second paragraph he begins to describe the many faces of love.

Let me lift up three of them, three that emerge gracefully out of these incredible and beloved words of scripture.

LOVE IS PATIENT AND KIND

Paul says that in verse 4, and then he describes what that means in the words that follow.

Love is patient and kind, or in other words, it's not jealous or boastful, not arrogant or rude, not selfish or closed-minded, not irritable or resentful.

Now, let me tell you something. We weren't born that way. We weren't born patient and kind. We all came into the world screaming, "Do something for me! Feed me, love me, hold me, burp me, change me, rock me," in any order you like and at any time you like, as long as it's right now!

Please don't misunderstand me. I love little babies. They are wonderful. They represent God's greatest miracle—the miracle of birth—and, as Carl Sandburg said, they represent God's affirmation that life should go on. But the truth is that they are born blinded by the cataracts of selfishness. They see every person as someone who exists solely for their benefit and comfort. That's the way babies are. They are not born patient and kind. They are born loveable, but they have to learn how to be loving.

Throughout infancy, childhood, the teen years (if nothing happens to convert them), and sometimes, sadly, even into adulthood, some people never mature. It's me, me, me. Take care of me. Do for me. Cater to me. Please me. Give to me. Pamper me. That kind of infantile, immature "me-ism" is so sad and tragic. It is what makes childish people jealous and boastful, arrogant and rude, irritable and resentful.

But Jesus first and later Paul bring us up short because they make it very clear that we have to be converted and redeemed, that we have to die to selfishness and be born again to love, that we have to give up our childish ways and take up the mature ways of Christ as God's self-giving servants in this world.

Here's the way it works. When Christ comes into your life, when the Spirit of Christ really takes residence in your heart, he makes you loving, patient, and kind. You become the instrument of his love and peace. Let me show you what I mean.

Have you heard the story about the famous violinist who was to give a concert in a certain city? He owned one of the finest Stradivarius violins in existence. For several days in advance of the concert, a number of news stories appeared in the local papers. The reporters downplayed the talent of the violinist, saying that he was not much more than an average musician, but what made him worth hearing was his extraordinary violin.

The morning of the concert there was a picture of the violin on the front page. That night the concert hall was crowded, a standing-room-only audience. The violinist came out and played. The music was exquisite, and at the end of the concert the audience gave a standing ovation.

Suddenly, the violinist did a strange thing. He walked over to a chair on the stage and smashed his violin across the back of the chair. Pieces flew everywhere. There was a gasp from the shocked audience. Then the violinist walked to the microphone and said to the people that he had read the stories about how his only claim to fame was his Stradivarius violin.

He then explained that earlier that day he had walked up the street to a local pawnshop. There he had bought a violin for five dollars. He had put some strings on it and played the concert that night not with his Stradivarius violin but with a five-dollar pawnshop violin! And that's the one he smashed. Then he said: "I know it disturbed you to see me smash this violin, but I just want you to know that the real music is not in the violin; it's in the violinist!"

The point is: when it comes to love, we may be like a cheap pawnshop violin, but in God's hands we can make beautiful music, the beautiful music of patience and kindness and love. First, love is patient and kind.

LOVE REJOICES IN WHAT IS RIGHT AND GOOD

In verse 6, Paul puts it like this: "[Love] does not rejoice in wrongdoing, but rejoices in the truth."

One of the best things we can do for children, for our families, for our friends, for our nation, and indeed for our world is to stand tall for righteousness. All across the globe today, people are starved to death for models of righteousness, for persons who commit their lives to goodness and justice and rejoice in what is right. That's one of the most loving things we can do: to live before others in the spirit of honesty and integrity and morality.

Sometimes it is hard to practice what we preach.

Have you heard about the unmarried man who went about the country giving a lecture on "Ten Commandments for Parents"? He was a very popular speaker and always drew a big crowd. In the midst of his fame, he fell in love and got married. After the arrival of their first baby, he changed the title of his talk to "Ten Suggestions for Parents." With a second baby, his talk was called "Ten Helpful Hints for

Parents." When a third child came, he stopped giving the talk altogether!

Sometimes it is difficult to live out the principles of life and faith that we sincerely believe and indeed want to practice. But no matter how demanding, we must not "throw in the towel." We must not quit on morality. We must not give up on righteousness.

Some years ago a man came to my office late one afternoon. He was deeply troubled and wanted to talk about his problem. He had just come from the local police station, where his teenage son had been taken into custody. The boy had been caught stealing some clothes from a large department store. The dad told me that he had been able to get his son out of jail after the boy received a strong reprimand from the police.

The father was, to put it mildly, very upset about what his son had done, but when they got in the car to go home, it got worse. The father said to his son,

"What were you thinking? You know better than that! Where on earth did you learn to steal like that?" The father was stunned and shocked by his son's answer. His son said, "From you!"

"From me?" the father stammered out. "What do you mean?"

The boy replied, "Dad, do you remember when I was five years old and I put a toy in my pocket at the toy store? When we got home and I showed it to you, you didn't take me back to return it. You thought it was funny. You thought it was cute. You just laughed and said, 'Well, it serves them right. They overcharge for everything, anyway.' That's what I was thinking about when I took those clothes today. I didn't have enough money, so I thought, *They are overcharging for these clothes, so I am just going to take them. It will serve them right*."

That dad was so embarrassed and so remorseful as

he realized painfully how one incident from years before had influenced his son in such a negative and detrimental way. And that dad made a solemn vow then and there to do everything in his power to rectify that situation.

That's a dramatic example, to be sure, but it is true (so true) that our children do indeed watch us closely and learn so much from what we do.

Now, let me ask you: What are your children today learning from you? Are they learning how to steal? how to deceive? how to scheme and trick and connive? how to rejoice in what is wrong? Or are they learning how to love? Are they learning from you how to be truthful and honest? how to care for others and respect them? how to rejoice in goodness and justice and righteousness?

First, love is patient and kind. Second, love rejoices in what is right and good.

LOVE IS THE MOST POWERFUL THING IN THE WORLD

The apostle Paul said, "[Love] bears all things, believes all things, hopes all things, endures all things. Love never ends. . . . Faith, hope, and love abide, these three; and the greatest of these [the most powerful of these] is love."

Not long ago a woman in her mid-forties was interviewed on television in Boston. She had a frightening story. In graphic detail, she described an extremely brutal childhood. A battered child, she had been beaten repeatedly and violently in every conceivable way by both her father and mother.

Even though she still has scars and terrible memories, amazingly she came out of that ordeal and rose above it. She is now happily married and has a highly responsible and productive career. When the woman was asked why she thought she had not only survived but triumphed over that horrible home situation, she answered, "I had more love than they had hate!"

So here they are—three good things we, as dads, need to constantly remember and to constantly teach our children:

- Love is patient and kind.
- Love rejoices in what is right and good.
- Love is the most powerful thing in the world.